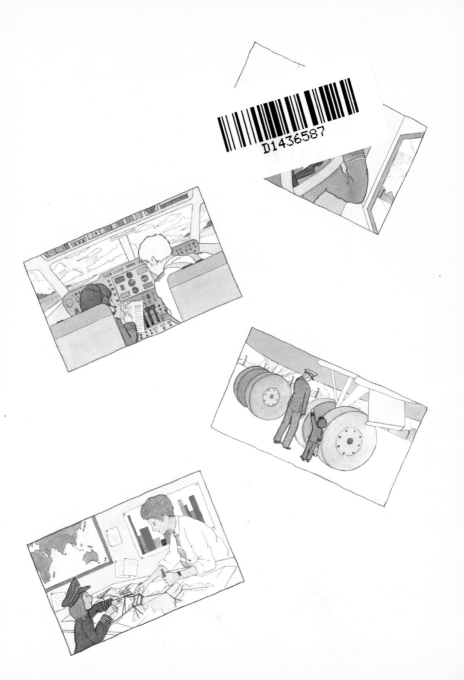

With special thanks to
Captain Patricia Richardson
and also to
Captain Jeff Bines
Air UK Ltd.

Published exclusively for
J Sainsbury plc
Stamford Street London SE1 9LL
by Walker Books Ltd
184 - 192 Drummond Street
London NW1 3HP

First published 1985
Reprinted 1985
© 1985 David Bennett

ISBN 0-7445-0442-2

PLAY · AND · LEARN

If I were a
Pilot

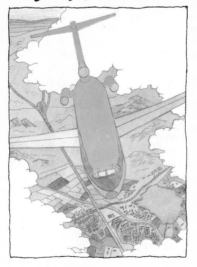

by
David Bennett

SAINSBURY'S · WALKER BOOKS

If I were a pilot I would
fly round the world.

Dressed in my uniform
of blue and gold...

I get to the airport

one hour before take-off,

check the route and weather,

look up my aircraft and its load.

Then I meet the crew.

My first officer will help me
fly the aircraft.

We all go out to the aircraft.

The first officer checks it
over with me.

In the cockpit

I put on my radio headphones.

There's lots of paperwork to do.

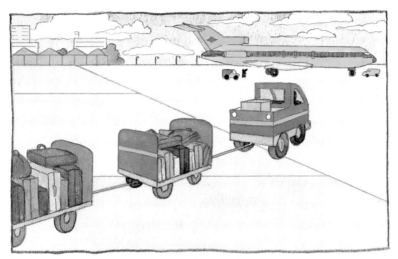

The luggage is loaded.

The passengers climb aboard.

Air traffic control tell me
I can start the engines.

Fasten your seat belts, please.

The doors are locked.
We taxi to the runway.

All through the flight

I keep checking the controls.

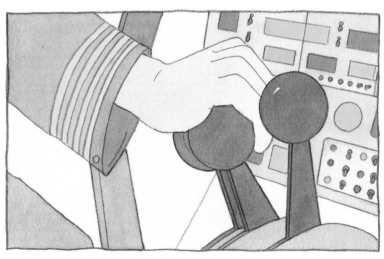

Throttles open, away we go!

Gathering speed...

faster and faster...

Whoosh! Down the runway...

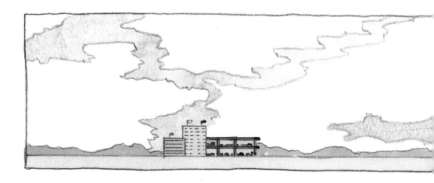

up...

up... and away!

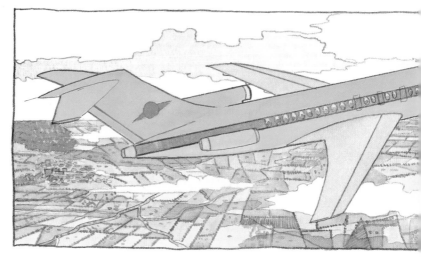

We fly over towns and fields,

up through the clouds

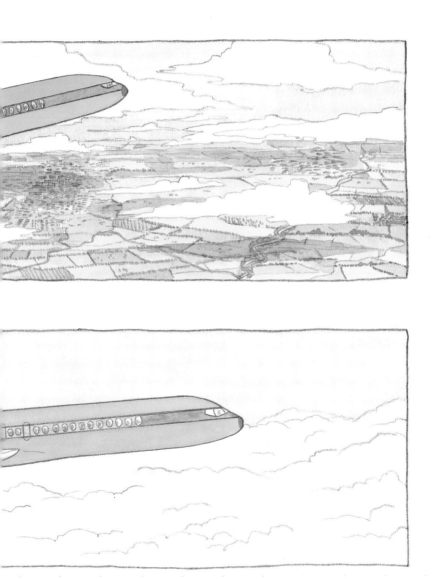

and into the blue.

Up in the air...

high over the sea...

the cabin crew serve food.

I speak to the passengers.

Ladies and gentlemen...

we are flying at 37,000 feet,

travelling at 500 miles per hour.

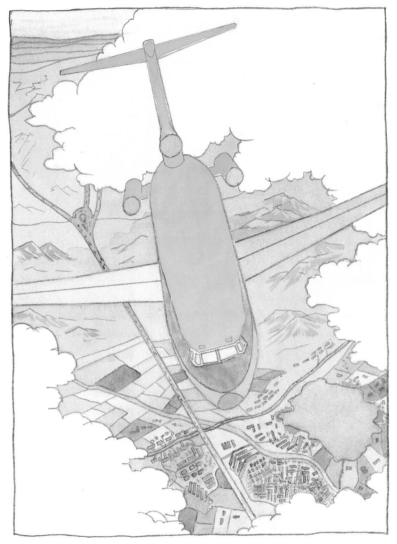

Soon we'll be coming in to land.

Air traffic control clear us for final approach to the runway.

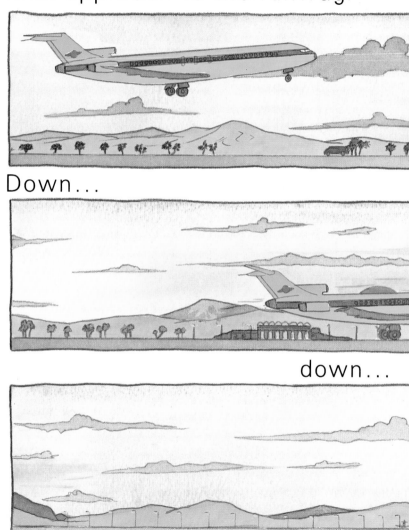

Down...

down...

... a perfect landing.

We arrive in a new country.

Passengers leave the aircraft.
For some of them it's home.

Next morning, another pilot
flies me home.

Tomorrow, maybe I'll be an
astronaut and fly to the moon.